DEEP
PSYCHOLOGICAL
NEEDS

Metropolitan Youssef

ST MARY & MOSES ABBEY PRESS

The Deep Psychological Needs
By Metropolitan Youssef

Copyright © 2023 Coptic Orthodox Diocese of the Southern U.S.A.

All rights reserved.

Designed & Published by:
St. Mary & St. Moses Abbey Press
101 S Vista Dr, Sandia, TX 78383
stmabbeypress.com

Translation from Arabic by St. Mary & St. Moses Abbey.

Contents

Introduction

Many problems and disagreements exist within a family, between a husband and wife. Therefore, marital problems are continually on the rise in Christian families.

This book presents a spiritual study, to [help] both the husband and wife discover the reasons leading them to these disagreements, and [discover] the deep psychological needs which every human being has and how to satisfy them within the family; and [discover] the complicated and deeply hidden issues, that form the sentiment and mind-set of each of us. These needs and issues are usually acquired in infancy or adolescence. Therefore, each one's reaction depends on these, when events take place and incidents are encountered in our daily life, and consequently, the shape and kind of the relationship with the other are defined through this reaction.

The human being's strong relationship with God, the study of the Holy Scriptures, and the practice of Church Mysteries, are a source of true satisfaction to every need God created within the human being. Therefore, the human being will not acquire inner peace and true joy and perfect love, except in the presence of the Lord Christ, by whom and to whom and in whom are all things.

1

Events and Issues

There are many events[1] that can result in many problems within the family. Buying something may be a reason for a major problem, because of the money spent on the purchase. So is the case for every action taken by one of the two sides.

There may be minor or major events, as [when] the husband discovers that his wife has spent a huge amount of money on buying something pricey, without telling him in advance. So, a major fight is enkindled between them on the wake of this. Or, it may be that one of them had forgotten to turn off the lights in the house, and though this may be a minor and petty event in itself, it also may be a cause of a fight breaking out between the two sides.

And from the start, I would like to differentiate

---

1   Or: occurrences.

between two things: events and issues[2] that are disagreed upon. Buying something is an event; this event, however, may set off a major problem around the issue of money and how to manage it, and how to plan a budget for the family, and the way on which the two sides agree to spend money in agreement. love and honesty. For when there are disagreements around the issue of money, we find that every event linked to money will create a problem. Conversely, when there is concord between the husband and wife, an atmosphere of goodwill will prevail in the family.

And the issues, out of which disagreements arise within a family, are numerous. The following are the most prominent [issues]:

1. **Money**: this includes all family-related monetary matters, including the sources of income, expenditures, and planning a budget, etc.

2. **Communication between the husband and wife**: the manner with which they talk with each other, and generally, among all the members of the family; and how they convey information; and [how they] exchange conversations and discuss all what concerns the family, in an atmosphere of honesty and concord.

3. **Children and the ways of bringing them up**: the husband may have a particular philosophy on bringing [children] up, and the wife, another

---

2   Or: Subject matter.

philosophy. And then, when an action is taken related to the upbringing of children, that is at odds with the partner's action, a fight might break out between them. For they have never agreed on a single course of action, accepted by both, to follow in bringing their children up.

4. **The marital and intimate relationship**: this may be a cause provoking many problems between the husband and wife.

5. **The big family**: that is, the husband's family or the wife's family. A phone call the husband makes with his mother may cause a big problem with his wife. And whenever there is any sort of communication between a spouse with his\her family, a big problem is set off between them. And if an agreement is not reached concerning how to deal with the big family, there will always be problems.

6. **Leisure**: where and how do they spend their leisure time; and do they go to a particular place or would the husband rather stay at home to watch a game or a movie, etc.

7. **Some undesirable habits**: smoking, for example, or drinking alcoholic beverages, or the bad use of the internet and television, and chatting rooms, etc. All these things may be a cause provoking disagreements between the spouses.

8. **Planning for the future**: the two sides having different visions (our career) may also cause

problems between the husband and wife.

9. **The Church and service**: these may be a cause of many problems between the husband and wife. For example, if the wife were active and diligent and attends weekly one of the servant meetings or were active in visitations, a problem might arise weekly between her and her husband who would accuse her of not devoting enough time for housework, and that this service keeps her busy away from him personally, and that she does not make enough time for him; and this event sets a problem off. And this indicates that the two sides had not reached an agreement regarding Church and the service.

10. **Housework**: many problems may also arise from housework and who is the one performing them.

In short, most of the problems arise from incidents and events of this sort, in addition to many others. Then an argument begins around these issues, and we find that rarely would the husband and wife sit together and discuss them.

The important question, however, which we have to lay out is: When do they discuss, and what is the most suitable time to begin the discussion? Is it when a particular event happens or [when] a problem surfaces intensely, that they sit and discuss this event or that problem? Of course, no, [not so].

If a wife, for example, discovered that her husband had bought something with a huge amount of money, should she start a fight with him on the issue of money? Is this the most suitable time for discussion? No, [not so].

These issues, in reality, touch the deep and innermost feelings within the human being, and rarely do we talk about them or reveal them. For example, a husband might complain that his wife spends a lot of time in service; and she might complain also that he is not religious and does not love God, and that he is far from Church which is why he does not want her to join the service. Nevertheless, he may be a religious person and has a relationship with God, and may love the Church and service; but he actually feels that his wife does not give him the attention he needs. And as we will see when we speak about our innermost feelings, this husband does not feel secure, and therefore he expresses his feelings in this manner, rather than saying frankly that he needs his wife to spend time with him and that she does not free this time for him; so he begins to provoke a problem, and a fight erupts between them wherein he blames her, that she goes out often and spends a long time serving in Church; [yet] the reason is that he cannot express his needs in a sound manner.

These issues sometimes conceal the deep and innermost feelings within the human being, which we rarely talk about. Therefore, we will, in the beginning, address the following important subject.

The Events, Issues, and Deep Feelings

As we have previously mentioned, some events may cause problems to blow up, at whose root are the hidden feelings which we do not express in a sound way. And perhaps the more accurate term for the hidden feelings is "the inner needs," which represent the roots out of which these issues emerge.

There are six essential needs within a family which have to be met. When they are not satisfied, from them issues will subsequently result which lead to many problems. These needs are the following:

1. The need of power and the love of having dominion and control.

2. The need of commitment or commitment to a relationship.

3. The need of love and care; the person feels that he is loved by the other, that the other person cares about him and about his needs, and takes care of him.

4. The need of faithfulness and integrity, meaning that the person is not two-faced. Rather, as he is on the inside, so he is also on the outside. His behavior does not reflect a different image to what is within him.

5. The need of appreciation; you feel that the other person appreciates and respects you.

6. The need of acceptance, meaning that the

human being feels that he is accepted by the other person.

We will speak in details on these six needs in the second chapter.

Dealing with Occurrences and Events

Most married couples have unresolved issues occupying their mind, yet they do not reveal them, nor do they talk to anyone about them until a particular event takes place. Only then do they begin raising these issues and talking about them, once an event has taken place, some of which we have previously presented, like the upbringing of children or some of the undesirable habits, etc. These issues are on our mind, but we do not talk about them until a problem explodes. And here I go back to the question I already put forth: Is the most suitable time to discuss this issue or that event immediately when it takes place?

This time is not suitable for discussion because of the feelings of anger which take hold of a person in these moments, and because the person focuses too closely on the event itself. As soon as the event takes place, I feel distressed and anger takes hold of me, so I begin focusing on the event itself, rather than the issue. For example, if the husband discovers that his wife has spent a large amount [of money], fierce anger takes hold of him and he begins yelling in her face, asking, "How did you spend such an amount?" Here, he focuses, in his conversation, on the event—that is, the spending of a large amount—rather than talking about the issue of money spending in general, [about] planning a policy for spending, and [about] how to deal, in general, with the family's monetary affairs.

These events, often, take place at times not suitable for constructive dialogue to resolve these issues; therefore, it is wise that we separate between these two things: Events and Issues.

Separating Between Events and Issues

When a particular event or an occurrence takes place, and I discover that it is agitating and distressing me very much, I have to deal with the event as something that actually took place. For example, the scenario which we previously related: the husband discovers that a large amount of money was spent by his wife. He has to deal with the occurrence only, which he is about to address, and should not at the moment go into the issue of money, that is, placing a policy and a plan for money spending in the family. He has to postpone speaking about it for another time, when he is prepared mentally to discuss the issue, having the goal of reaching satisfactory solutions. Often naturally, we may have a burning desire to bring up the incident and discuss it immediately. This inclination may lead to crises and problems difficult to resolve, especially when we are agitated, and we would hurt each other. Also the problem will become aggravated and bigger. And instead of it being a problem only of money or raising children or difference in opinion, it becomes transformed into a series of layered problems of hurting each other's feelings, of insults, of anger on both sides, in addition to it being originally a problem of money spending.

There is more than one issue needing a solution, and we will not be able to reach solutions if the time is not suitable or if we are in a hurry. Also the other person may have the feeling that we are controlling him and that we do not want to listen to his opinion. Therefore, it is important that we understand the deep feelings which we are about to deal with.

Choosing a Suitable Time

The Holy Scripture teaches us: "To everything there is a season, a time for every purpose under heaven... A time to keep silence, and a time to speak."[3] The meaning of this is that there is a time for speaking and a time for remaining silent. Wisdom tells us that this time is not a time for speaking; rather let the event pass in peace. That is, do not talk about it as soon as it happens. Returning to the previous example regarding money, the husband may say, "I am not comfortable about the way money was

---

3   Ecclesiastes 3:1,7.

15

spent, and we need to sit together to discuss this issue and to place a policy for it, so that we do not fall into this problem again. But the time is not suitable right now; therefore, we can postpone it to another time tomorrow." When the time is suitable and the husband and wife are in a state of calmness and serenity, [only] then can they discuss the issue.

Yes, you may, simply, express your discomfort regarding what happened, but you will postpone talking about it to the future.

Make an Appointment to Discuss the Issue

It is necessary that an appointment is made to discuss the issue. Otherwise, the husband and wife will always be living on a minefield, and irritation will prevail at all times in their life. Appointing a suitable time depends on their readiness to talk about the issue. Perhaps, you think that what I am saying is unrealistic or idealistic. But believe me that this is the [best] way with which we can resolve our problems, because when we get agitated, and our voices are raised, and we fight, the result is [more] problems, and enmity, and hurt feelings; and we reach no solution. If both sides, however, are able to control themselves, and they express their discomfort regarding what had happened, and they appoint [a specific] time to discuss it, this will effectively influence [their] reaching a resolution for the problem.

There are people, of course, who do not like

to use this method. We have to, however, bear the responsibility when there exists an issue causing discomfort to one of the sides. They have to discuss [it] with love, concord and honesty. This has to start with a prayer, so that the Holy Spirit may overshadow them, and they should not end their meeting before reaching a suitable solution that satisfies both sides. Without this, we are continually living on a field full of mines. And every event becomes like a mine buried in the ground, so if we step on it, it explodes, and therefore problems will never end, and the husband and wife will not enjoy peace. Though they may have a period of calmness, it is temporary, because the mine will explode whenever an event takes place.

But the important question is: How do we deal with the issues, and how do we resolve the problems? I have previously spoken about the difference between an event and an issue. This point I would like to focus on, because I cannot discuss the issues when a particular event sets them off. When an event takes place, we have to deal with it objectively and calmly, and appoint a time in which we are ready and mentally prepared to talk about the issue resulting from it, to be able to reach an agreement on how to deal with it in the future.

"We need to know when to remain silent and when to speak, and how to remain silent and what to say."

—Saint Isaac the Syrian—

2

The Hidden and Deep Feelings

Although it is easy to recognize the issues that are set off by events, there are sometimes problems that result from trifling events, which do not [in truth] deserve to be a problem. Consequently, it may be difficult to recognize the issue causing the problem. And the married couple might not know a reason for what had happened, and might ask, "We want to know why this disagreement and dispute happened." They then discover that the cause of the incident which they are talking about, is considered a very insignificant thing, but it led to a disagreement and contention.

The Hidden Feelings

It may be difficult to diagnose the issue causing the disagreement, and the husband and wife may discover that the reasons are very insignificant, but, in reality, there are many things between them, and these things are buried and they cannot [easily] discover them or distinguish them. Therefore, they appear in the form of disagreements and disputes over trifling matters. And here, these hidden feelings, which we call the deep needs, are the cause of the problem.

We call them "the hidden feelings" because, often, they do not emerge to the surface in conversations, despite their importance. For example, an argument might erupt, or a disagreement might break out between a husband and wife over a button in the shirt. But this is not the principal cause at the moment. The principal cause is the existence of hidden feelings within him; for he feels that she does not love him. Therefore, when we discover these feelings present within us, recognize them, and then we talk about them in an atmosphere of love and honesty and acceptance, the problems, resulting from the trifling issues, will [consequently] disappear.

The Deep Psychological Needs

There are six deep needs or inner feelings which we will address with explanation and analysis. And these are:

First: The Need of Power and the Love of Authority

Does any of the sides feel that their freedom is lost, or that one of them wants to have the upper hand? This need is the first thing that comes to the husband's and wife's mind, even if they do not disclose it. There are many questions that swarm the mind of each of them. For example: Are my wishes, my needs, my opinions, important to the other person? Who has the last word at home? Do I participate in making decisions, or does the other person insist on doing their opinion? Does the husband reject every decision taken by the wife, yet he continues in arguing and discussing with the wife until she is so aggravated that she gives her consent [to his opinion]? The husband, consequently, announces that she had consented, but internally he does not feel that she [really] consented but she did so to stop arguing forever. Does everything have to be under your control as a husband, and you feel distressed if there is something which is not subject to your control?

A verse in the Epistle to the Ephesians, is quoted[4] by many husbands. The verse is, "Wives, submit to your own husbands, as to the Lord." The love of controlling is made manifest in our dealings within the family, but with love and humility the husband and wife can work [together] as a team. We read the epistle of our teacher Paul the Apostle to the Ephesians in the Crowning Prayer: "Wives, submit to your own husbands, as to the Lord. For the husband

4   Literally: used.

is head of the wife, as also Christ is head of the church; and He is the Savior of the body."[5] It teaches us about love and submission, and asks the wives to be subject to their own husbands as to the Lord, and asks the husbands to love their wives as Christ also loved the church and gave Himself for her sake. Does the Holy Spirit mean in this that wives are asked to be subject to their husbands without [the wives] having love, or that the husbands are asked to love their wives yet [the husbands] are not asked to submit? Imagine with me, if the man were to love but not to submit, meaning that he does not discuss with his wife nor take her opinion; likewise, if the woman were to submit without offering love, how would the relationship between them look like? This is not the Christian relationship God intended for the church, for the relationship of the church with Christ is a relationship of love and submission. This is [exactly] what the Lord wants within the family.

A person, perhaps, may ask, saying, "It is true that the Lord Christ loves the church, and that the church loves the Lord Christ and is subject to Him, so can we say that the Lord Christ is subject to the church, and how can this be?"

It is undoubtedly difficult to accept this statement, that the Lord Christ is subject to the church. But when we meditate on some of the stories that came in the Holy Scriptures, we can understand

---

5   Ephesians 5:22–23.

this matter.

The Lord said to Abraham, "Shall I hide from Abraham what I am doing"?[6] Then the discussion begins between God and Abraham regarding the destruction of Sodom and Gomorrah. So Abraham says to the Lord, "Would You also destroy the righteous with the wicked?... Far be it from You! Shall not the Judge of all the earth do right?" The words Abraham said to the Lord are rough, but the Lord accepted this objection, and He came to terms with Abraham: "If I find in Sodom fifty righteous within the city, then I will spare all the place for their sakes." And Abraham would bargain with the Lord: "Suppose there were five less than fifty righteous," "Suppose there should be forty found there," until he reached to ten [righteous people]. The Lord took Abraham's opinion in consideration and went for it. This illustrates how the Lord deals with the church which is represented in the person of Abraham.

The same thing happened with Moses. The Lord said to Moses, "Now therefore, let Me alone, that My wrath may burn hot against them and I may consume them."[7] It is as though Moses is preventing the Lord from consuming the children of Israel. It says:

Then Moses pleaded with the LORD his God, and said: "LORD, why does Your

---

6   See Genesis 18:17–33.

7   See Exodus 32:7–14.

wrath burn hot against Your people whom
You have brought out of the land of Egypt
with great power and with a mighty hand?
Why should the Egyptians speak, and say,
'He brought them out to harm them, to kill
them in the mountains.'"[8]

Here [we see] the Lord taking Moses' opinion.
This is the concept of intercession, the intercession
of the church and the saints for His children.
The Lord takes the opinion of the church in His
consideration.

Who says that the love of having control is an
absolute right, that the woman is required only to
submit, and that the man is not required to take
her opinion? Many times the Lord says to Abraham,
"Whatever Sarah has said to you, listen to her voice."[9]
Yes, the commandment to submit is directed to
women, and [the commandment to] love is directed
to men, but this does not grant men authority, nor
does it command women to only submit. It came,
however, to satisfy a need in the man and woman,
for the woman's principal need is the feeling of being
loved—because she is sentimental—but she also
has a need of being respected and appreciated. The
principal need in man is respect and appreciation,
but he also has a need of being loved.

Out of this came the commandment, "Wives,

---

8   Exodus 32:11–12.

9   Genesis 21:12.

submit to your own husbands ... Husbands, love your wives,"[10] to satisfy their inner deep needs according to the psychological formation of the man and the psychological formation of the woman. Paul the Apostle says, "Submitting to one another in the fear of God."[11] Submission, here, means concord, dialogue, and working together as a team. And this will not take place except through love and true humility. As St. Anthony says, "Love and humility subdue[12] wild beasts," meaning that love and humility can subdue even those who have the temperament of wild beasts.

Our past experiences from our childhood may be a reason for the hypersensitivity of one of the two sides, and consequently [the person] may always interpret the actions of the other in a negative way, that the person is controlling. For example, the husband may ask his wife to get him a cup of water. This simple request, however, may be the cause of a huge problem. She may answer him, saying, "Why don't you get it yourself? Am I your servant? What! Did you buy me?" The request, in reality, is not the root of the problem; the principal reason is that she has an inward, buried feeling that her husband is controlling her. Therefore, any small request made in the form of an order, sets off in her the feelings that her husband is controlling her, even though the

---

10   Ephesians 5:22,25.

11   Ephesians 4:21.

12   The Arabic word used is a derivative of the word "submit."

reaction does not match at all the event [or incident] that took place; the issue of "get me a cup of water" is not the problem. But it is this statement [spoken by the husband] which nurtures in her the idea and inward feeling that her husband is controlling her; therefore, she refuses to submit to even these small requests.

I would like here to point to [the fact] that the love of authority and dominion has two aspects. The first aspect is that the person wants actually to be in control of all matters and to exercise dominion over everything. The second aspect is that one of the two sides may have suffered in childhood from the control of their father or mother, and therefore, they may be hypersensitive regarding the issue of authority and control. This hypersensitivity shows up whenever any order is directed to them. Problems consequently take place although the other side may not be dominating or controlling.

The love of being controlling reflects selfishness

Where do wars and fights come from among you? Do they not come from your desires for pleasure that war in your members? You lust and do not have. You murder and covet and cannot obtain. You fight and war. Yet you do not have because you do not ask. You ask and do not receive, because you ask amiss, that you may spend it on your pleasures.[13]

---

13   James 4:1–3.

The love of authority reflects a sort of selfishness within the person, meaning that he only cares about his own interests and his own opinion, regardless of the interest and opinion of the other side. Our teacher James the Apostle says, "Where do wars and fights come from among you? Do they not come from your desires for pleasure that war in your members?" This is what [actually] happens in the world. The reason for wars between countries and fights between people, is selfishness. Each person desires to control the other. And he says too, "You lust and do not have." I have a desire[14] and make war to fulfill it... Our teacher James continues, saying, "You murder and covet and cannot obtain. You fight and war. Yet you do not have because you do not ask. You ask and do not receive, because you ask amiss, that you may spend it on your pleasures."

If one of the two sides has suffered from past experiences, this may make the person hypertensive, and consequently, the person evaluates the other's actions in a negative way—that is, the other is controlling—so how do we deal with such a situation?

Negative interpretation produces mistrust between the husband and wife

Negative interpretation, undoubtedly, produces a sort of mistrust between a husband and wife. When

---

14   The word in Arabic is the noun of the word "lust" in the verse.

the wife interprets every action in a negative manner, that her husband is controlling and dominating, there will come a time wherein she feels mistrust toward him or in the honesty of his intentions. He, likewise, will feel mistrust toward her also, and this will create a gap between them, and day after day this gap will grow wider[15]. This matter requires that each understands the other person, and deals with the other kindly and tenderly, until trust is established between them.

The question is, "What do we do in such an event?" Let us consider the hurt person, due to past experiences which made him hypersensitive in this manner, as a weak person; and that the other person, who is wrongly understood, as being controlling and dominating though he may not be so, as the strong person. So what does Holy Scripture say here? "We then who are strong ought to bear with the scruples of the weak, and not please ourselves."[16]

This means that the strong side must treat the weak side kindly and tenderly, until trust is established, which is the basis of every successful marriage. The strong side should not take these accusations personally, but that they are due to the hypersensitivity of the other side. When he deals with the other person with meekness and kindness, this hypersensitivity will begin to dissipate, and love

---

15   Literally: deeper.
16   Romans 15:1.

and honesty [will begin] to prevail.

[The love of] power is usually revealed in disagreements around money or in taking decisions [regardless of] whether minor or major. There is a relationship between money and power, for the people who are excessively careful about money often have hidden issues, which are power and the love of authority. Therefore, the husband may begin settling accounts with his wife with exactitude; or it may be that the wife accuses her husband of not covering the home's basic expenses.

Finally, in a nutshell, all disagreements and fights between a husband and wife may be due to a hidden feeling of needing to control and a love of authority.

Second: The Need of Love and Care

Every one of us has a need of feeling loved and that others care about him. If this need is not satisfied, disputes, problems and fights will arise over insignificant, trifling matters.

If [such] thoughts become stirred in your mind as, "I feel that no one loves me," or, "I am useless at home; the kids are always talking with their mother! But no one ever talks with me," if the matter is so, all of your emotional needs may not be satisfied.

Let us think about Adam whom God created and placed in paradise. He did not experience any of the distresses and problems which we now face; there were no expenses or bills to pay, there were no children to raise, nor was there anybody to fight with or control. Nevertheless, Adam was not feeling at rest, though everything was available for him, and though he was with God, being master over the whole creation. Adam did have a need, however: he needed a person like him, who is of flesh, body, and spirit, who may love and commune with him, that he may feel loved and cared about. Because God knew that Adam had this need, He did not blame him, but, on the contrary, He said, "It is not good that man should be alone,"[17] so He created Eve for him.

> *"As a child, terrified by some frightening sight, runs to its parents, clutches the hem of their garments, and cries out to them, so too with the soul; for the more she is straightened and afflicted by fear arising from temptations, the more she hastens to cleave to God, crying out to Him with continual supplication."[18]*

> —Saint Isaac the Syrian—

---

17   Genesis 2:18.

18   *The Ascetical Homilies of Saint Isaac the Syrian.* (Boston, MS: Holy Transfiguration Monastery, 2011), 510–511.

We all have the need of being loved and cared about by the other person

Disagreements around insignificant[19] matters are caused by a hidden feeling that the other person does not love me or care about me. A huge fight might break out over trifling matters, because this need is not satisfied.

For example, if the husband does not find something to eat on returning home, a fight would break out with his wife, even though food [itself] does not represent a problem for him because he can prepare food for himself; and perhaps he used to do this before getting married. The issue leading to the fight appears on the outside to be over food, but it truly touches on a deep need in him, that he is not loved, and therefore, his wife does not care about him.

Here is another example: A wife starts a fight with her husband because he did not remember her birthday and did not give her a gift. In [outward] appearance the fight is due to the [husband's] forgetting and not giving her a gift. The husband may also say, "You are materialistic and you want me to get you a gift." And it may not be so, but the main reason is that the gift satisfies a need within her, which is: Her husband loves her, cares about her, and cares about her feelings.

---

19   Literally: simple.

Why do we usually avoid talking about this need?

1. Pride

We do not talk about this need present in us when we often feel insecure; so we do not express it. But this need is made manifest in the form of problems over trifling matters. One of the reasons making people feel insecure to talk about this need is pride. We think that talking about this matter will come across as weakness. The wife may say, "Do I have to beg for his love?" And the husband may feel that this matter is against his self-esteem and his pride, so he may say, "I do not need this thing from her."

When we, however, do not express this need, clearly and faithfully, these needs will nevertheless become manifest, as we have previously said, in the form of problems over trifling matters. Talking about our needs, however, in a safe atmosphere and honestly will end many disagreements over insignificant matters.

2. The anxiety over the other's reaction

There is another reason that makes us avoid talking about our needs, and especially about this need; that is, we do not know how the other person will react. For example, when the wife talks to her husband about her need for affection, love and tenderness, and the husband dismisses this need as unimportant—and he may say to her things like,

"Aren't we too old for this.[20]?"—this response makes her think twice before revealing what is on her mind and before talking about her needs, because her husband's response hurt her feelings, so she fears that he would hurt her again.

But what do we mean by talking about the need of love and care in a safe atmosphere? It means that I can talk and reveal all my needs to the other person without fearing the [other's] reaction. When this takes place, we can express our needs; and when we talk about them, reveal them, and [when consequently] they are satisfied, disagreements and problems resulting from small trifling matters will be diminished; and the husband and wife will feel that they love each other. And if the husband is utterly sure of his wife's love for him, then when he returns home and does not find food [ready], he will find excuses for her. He will say to himself, "Maybe she was tired, or [maybe] she is not feeling well," and will begin preparing food for himself, feeling joyful because he is helping his wife and giving her comfort. The wife, likewise, when she feels that her husband loves and cares about her, she will not stir up disagreements and problems over the remembering of days and dates, and over not receiving gifts.

The need of love and care may be a hidden need within us, but is made manifest in the form of

---

20   Literally: are we still young?

insignificant problems and disagreements.

Third: The Need of Appreciation

Sometimes a person may think to himself, saying, "I wonder if the other person appreciates me? Or does he appreciate what I do for him, working hard in it? Does he appreciate me for who I am, or he appreciates me for my finances & expenditures?"

Many men may complain that their wives do not appreciate the hard work they do. Instead of hearing a word of appreciation from his wife, she may say to him, "All men work; do you think you are the only one?" Likewise, many wives also do not feel the appreciation of their husbands for the work they do, whether it be housework or their careers. And the wife who does not have a job may hear her husband saying to her, "What do you do? All day long you are at home." Here they start comparing between what he does and what she does. These comparisons indicate a lack of appreciation for each other.

The Lord Christ commanded us to serve each other in love

There is a teaching advising that we should not direct a word of praise [to anyone] to avoid provoking the demons against the person. This teaching is correct; therefore, we find that the husband does not say a word of praise to his wife, nor does the wife say a word of appreciation to her husband, even though we all have a need for appreciation and praise. What is meant by this teaching, however, is the exaggeration in praising [someone], in fear that it may spoil the person, and consequently provoking the demons against the person. However, it is wrong that we do not say words of praise and encouragement at all, and it is not in accord with the teaching of Holy Scriptures. Paul the Apostle praised Timothy, mentioning his zeal and his toil. He also says to the church of the Thessalonians, "Remembering without ceasing your work of faith, labor of love, and patience of hope in our Lord Jesus Christ in the sight of our God and Father,"[21] and he praises the Philippians, saying, "Nevertheless you have done well that you shared in my distress. Now you Philippians know also that in the beginning of the gospel, when I departed from Macedonia, no church shared with me concerning giving and receiving but you only,"[22] and he praises Philemon for his love, [saying], "For we have great joy and consolation in your love, because the hearts of the saints have been refreshed by you, brother,"[23]etc. So, it is not always right if we follow the teaching that we should not praise anyone to avoid provoking the demons against them, and consequently that no words of praise and appreciation come out of our mouths to anyone, because everyone has a need for

---

21　1 Thessalonians 1:3.

22　Philippians 4:14–15.

23　Philemon 1:7.

encouragement and praise. We only need to stay away from exaggerating in doing so. We have to be spiritually balanced.

The Lord Christ commanded us to serve one another in love, and I believe that one of the most important forms of our serving one another in love is appreciation.

Each person must feel the other's appreciation for the work he is doing and the effort he is giving.

When the wife, who has a job outside, in addition to the housework, which she does after returning from work, feels that her husband fully appreciates the effort she is giving; and when the husband feels his wife's appreciation for the hard work he does to provide a good life for his family, then the bond of love between them will be strengthened, boosted and intensified.

When was the last time you said to the other person that you appreciate their hard work and their presence in your life? Each of the husband and wife should remember the last time when they expressed to each other that each one appreciates the hard work and effort the other is doing, and that the other's presence means a lot in one's life. If the feelings of being appreciated have no place in our life, many problems will arise due to trifling reasons, and agitation will prevail in all the actions of the husband because of the lack of appreciation for his service and effort. This will end up by them casting the blame at each other: "She does not do anything," and "he does not say anything [good]," and so, fights break out between them.

Fourth: The Need of Commitment and Stability

By this need is meant family stability and commitment to the marriage covenant; that is, each of them should feel that their relationship is permanent and stable with the other person, and should not have fear that [the other] might separate from them and leave them at any moment.

Disagreements around having separate [bank] accounts are due to feeling unsafe and unsettled, and this perhaps happens frequently in the West and the United States, [but] rarely does it happen in Egypt. When problems happen between a husband and wife, the idea of divorce comes to their mind and they find many excuses for it; therefore, they say that this is the best solution for them and that God is not pleased by their suffering. The truth, however, is that the lack of stability in the marriage or the feeling that the other [person] might leave at any moment, threaten the family peace, and [consequently] leading to problems over trifling matters. And perhaps the problem happens because of the desire to separate their [bank] accounts, and each of them having an independent account. When we go deeper in analyzing this problem, we perhaps find that the reason is [linked to] what had happened in the husband's family when he was young: his mother, as a first step, had asked to separate her account from his father's, and in the second step, they separated from each other, then, in the subsequent step, divorce took place between them. Therefore, it was settled in the husband's mind that separating the accounts is nothing but a step toward divorce. Therefore, a huge fight might happen because of accounts' separation, but, in reality, the husband has buried feelings which made him feel unsafe and unsettled, that his wife was doing this because she was planning on leaving him.

An agreement before marriage (prenuptial)

For this reason, there are people who make an agreement between them [before getting married] which is called pre-marital agreement [commonly known as prenup]. This means that the husband and wife sign in court a document, an agreement that in case of separation or divorce, they will split their possessions of money and property according to the manner they have agreed upon. They do this because most divorce-related problems revolve around splitting the money and possessions and around the place where the children will stay after divorce. This agreement ensures that, in the case that a divorce takes place, there will be no problems, nor will huge amounts of money be spent on lawyers.

There is another reason [for such agreements] which perhaps [mainly] concerns the wealthy. The wealthy husband cannot guarantee whether his wife married him for his person or for his money and possessions; therefore, he makes her sign a document wherein she makes a pledge that she gets nothing in the case of a divorce.

This agreement is undoubtedly utterly rejected in Christianity, because there is no divorce in Christianity, and consequently there is no need for making such an agreement. We reject that marriage be based on an agreement of this sort, and we advise our daughters living in the West and [the United States of] America to refuse signing such an agreement, because this agreement is against the teaching of the Church and presents a grave danger. There is no agreement whatsoever in Christianity on divorce. I reiterate: this thing is utterly rejected. Trust between the husband and wife is the foundation of Christian marriage. It is rather better not to get married to a person who does not trust the other person.

What is God's wisdom in making marriage a covenant and not a contract?

The covenant cannot be broken nor dissolved except by death, but a contract may be rescinded at any moment. When the Lord spoke in Malachi about marriage, He used the word "covenant" and not "contract."[24] Many people think that the absence [of

---

24   See Malachi 2:14.

the possibility] of divorce restricts their freedom, but this is not true. The absence of divorce, however, ensures the stability of the family, making you feel at peace, because, regardless of what happens, the relationship will remain in place. But if the wife feels that her husband can divorce her on a whim[25], there will be no stability whatsoever. Out of God's love for us, there is no divorce in the Christian marriage.

Many children whose parents were divorced harbor this fear in their own marriage

The children of the divorced [parents] harbor, unfortunately, a fear of instability in their own marriage. Children pay the highest price as a result of the divorce [of their parents]. Their suffering may continue, and their wounds may last, which were generated by their parents' divorce, even after their own marriage. The husband may feel that his wife could leave him any moment for the most trivial reasons, and so is the case with the wife.

I do remember once that a husband asked his wife in front of me personally the following question: "How long will you stay with me?" The reason is the absence of the sense of safety in the marriage.

Five: The Need of Uprightness and Integrity

By this we mean that the person is the same within

---

25   Literally: with a word.

and without, so that we do not appear as one thing while we are scheming something else [within]. For example, one person may have suspicion in the truthfulness of the intentions and motives of the other, or that one person may feel that the other person is doing him wrong by analyzing his actions and behavior.

On many occasions, [when] I sat with married couples, the husband would say to me, "Your Grace, do not believe her; she is making a show before you. She appears like an angel in front of you, but she is not like this in truth." So the wife would respond, [saying], "This is not right!" I would be saying [to myself], "I wonder which one of them is not straightforward and has no integrity," for things do not appear as they really are. Sometimes the reason for this suspicion which goes on between them is the lack of love or an act of projection. The husband who is not straightforward might accuse the wife of being not straightforward also, and so the wife would feel wronged. And the husband might perceive all her actions and behavior in a negative way, and thus problems float to the surface.

And if the husband notices that his wife is giving him extra attention, he would think to himself, saying, "Surely she wants something. [Maybe] she wants me to buy her a ring, or a dress..." and in this manner he explains all her actions. And he might ask her, "What are your demands today?" So she answers, "I do not need anything." And a fight breaks out between them because he has suspicion in the truthfulness of her intentions and straightforwardness.

It is not wise that we discuss or judge the intentions and actions of the other.

> But with me it is a very small thing that I should be judged by you or by a human court. In fact, I do not even judge myself. For I know of nothing against myself, yet I am not justified by this; but He who judges me is the Lord. Therefore judge nothing before the time, until the Lord comes, who will both bring to light the hidden things of darkness and reveal the counsels of the hearts. Then each one's praise will come from God.[26]

Speak only about the facts and events, and not your analysis of the actions and the personality of the other person, for no one can judge what is within except God and the person himself. Many of the problems arise from feeling that the other person has suspicion in the truthfulness of my intentions. We cannot judge the motives of a person. There were many in the church of Corinth who had suspicion in the calling of Paul the Apostle, so how did the Apostle deal with this matter? He said, "But with me it is a very small thing that I should be

---

26   1 Corinthians 4:3–5.

judged by you or by a human court."[27] So what did he mean by "a human court"? It is as though he was saying to them, "Are you holding a human trial [to decide] if I am an Apostle or not?" And do you have suspicion in the truthfulness of my intentions? I do not judge myself either, "for I know of nothing against myself, yet I am not justified by this; but He who judges me is the Lord."[28] Then he gave them an advice, saying, "Judge nothing before the time, until the Lord comes, who will both bring to light the hidden things of darkness and reveal the counsels of the hearts. Then each one's praise will come from God."[29]

Do not judge the other person; rather, deal with him in love, for love thinks no evil. Make sure that you interpret the other's actions in positive way. There are many who claim that they have the superpower of [being able to] understand personalities and to probe their depths; and this understanding, which they claim, may be wrong. Therefore, Holy Scripture advises us to judge nothing before the time[30]. If the wife cared about her husband in truth, and he felt the sincerity of her care, there would not be interpretations and analyses of the motives and intentions, which lead to problems and cause disturbance to both. "For what man knows the

---

27   1 Corinthians 4:3.

28   1 Corinthians 4:4.

29   1 Corinthians 4:5.

30   Ibid.

things of a man except the spirit of the man which is in him?"[31] Regardless of the degree of shrewdness and intelligence we are given, we should not claim that we know the motives of the other.

Six: The Need of Acceptance

The feeling of being accepted is extremely important. It is intertwined with all the previously-mentioned needs and emotions. If I felt that the other accepts me, I would not have a fear of being controlled and subjugated, and I would also feel loved and cared for. So is the case regarding uprightness and integrity, that I would not feel that the other person is acting deceptively toward me, but [I would feel that] his outward appearance reflects what is on the inside. If the other person accepts me, I will feel that he appreciates me, and will not fear that he will leave me one day.

Therefore, we say that this need is very important, and we have to help the other person feel accepted. We will speak in some detail about this essential need.

Many married people are afraid of feeling rejected; therefore, they build a wall to hide behind. What does the person do if he feels that he is not accepted by the other? Out of fear of rejection, he begins building a wall to hide behind, so that his

---

31   1 Corinthians 2:11.

feelings are not hurt, like what happened in the story of Adam after the fall. Holy Scripture says: Adam and Eve were both naked, yet felt no shame,[32] because nakedness here means that I am open[33]; that is, all my thoughts, feelings, fears, and weaknesses, are bare. Here, who I am in truth is made manifest before the other person, without being ashamed or having the feeling that the other person might reject me.

Who of us has the readiness to stand before everyone, to reveal everything in our life, that is, to reveal ourselves and our nakedness? It is unlikely that anyone of us would do this. Why? Because I want to be accepted, and I am afraid that if I uncover myself in this manner, the others will reject me; therefore, I would rather hide myself.

This was not the human being's state before the fall. They were in a state of innocence. Therefore, Adam and Eve were [both] naked, yet felt no shame. But what happened after their fall?

Holy Scripture says, "Then the eyes of both of them were opened, and they knew that they were naked; and they sewed fig leaves together and made themselves coverings."[34] When they felt naked and shame after [falling into] sin, and [felt] the fear of being rejected, they began hiding themselves behind

---

32   See Genesis 3:7–10.

33   Or: uncovered.

34   Genesis 3:7.

fig leaves.

Sometimes when I feel that the other person might reject me, I begin to hide behind fig leaves. I am afraid of revealing myself and of expressing myself in fear that the others might reject me. I am afraid of speaking honestly about what I am thinking about and what I believe in, in fear that people might reject me; I am afraid of expressing my feelings and needs. So, the feeling of being accepted is nonexistent [in my life].

Many of us do not speak about the previously-mentioned five needs in fear of being rejected.

As an example, the wife might be afraid to speak to her husband about her concerns that he is controlling her and exercises authority over her, so she starts a fight with him, and a big problem takes place between them. The reason behind all this is that there is a fear taking hold of her, that she should not express her feelings, to avoid being rejected. And as long as there is fear, there is no love, for "there is no fear in love; but perfect love casts out fear."[35] If there is acceptance, however, the other person will understand what I am saying and expressing.

The feeling of being accepted helps the person to be as he [truly] is and to behave naturally, and this creates a strong and tight bond between the

---

35   1 John 4:18.

husband and wife.

The feeling of rejection makes us express our needs indirectly

Of the effects resulting from a person feeling not accepted by the other, is the expression of his need in an indirect way. For example, a wife might say to her husband, "Would you like to do this?" And this is instead of saying frankly, "I would like to do this." And instead of the husband saying to his wife, "I need to spend the day with you,"—for he perhaps thinks that the word "I need" may make him appear weak, and he feels that if he said it, his wife would not treat him with dignity in the future, or this might diminish her respect for him, or she might reject his request—therefore, he substitutes the statement "I need to spend the day with you," with "Do you want to go out today?" She might answer him, [saying], "No, I am busy today!" He thinks that by doing this he shields himself, because he cannot express his need frankly; therefore, he makes a projection, saying, "She is the one who said 'No.'" The fear of rejection makes many of us express our needs indirectly.

Accepting one another is a biblical commandment

If this were a commandment directed to all people, it is more so directed to a married couple. Our teacher Paul the Apostle says, "Therefore receive[36]

---

36 This word also means "accept," but it appears as "receive" in NKJV.

one another, just as Christ also received us, to the glory of God."[37]

One of the most powerful examples showing the acceptance of the Lord Christ of us, is the story of the right-hand thief. At the start, the right-hand thief reviled the Lord Christ. In the Gospel according to our teacher Mark, it says, "Even those who were crucified with Him reviled Him."[38] And suddenly, when the right-hand thief saw the earthquake which took place, and when he heard the words of the Lord Christ which were full of love and forgiveness,—"Father, forgive them, for they do not know what they do,"[39]—his heart was moved and he said, "This is the Son of God in truth," and he began proclaiming the kingdom of the Lord Christ, His second coming, and His Divinity.

Many say that this thief had done no good deeds. This thief, however, confessed his sins and said to his friend, "Do you not even fear God, seeing you are under the same condemnation? And we indeed justly, for we receive the due reward of our deeds; but this Man has done nothing wrong."[40] Then he confessed the Divinity of the Lord Christ when he said, "Lord, remember me,"[41] and he confessed the kingdom of Christ, and that He is the King, when

---

37 Romans 15:7.
38 Mark 15:32.
39 Luke 23:34.
40 Luke 23:40–41.
41 Luke 23:42.

he said, "when You come into Your kingdom."[42] And he also confessed the second coming of the Lord Christ.[43]

The thief did many [good] deeds, at a time when all the disciples had fled. He confessed courageously the Lord Christ. Every word he was saying caused him excruciating bodily pain, for the sufferings of the cross were brutal. But when the Lord heard the words of this thief who, moments earlier, was reviling Him along with the other thief, He offered him love and acceptance, so He said to him, "Assuredly, I say to you, today you will be with Me in Paradise."[44]

Sometimes, when I am tired or exhausted or sick, and someone approaches me, I show him my lack of acceptance at that moment. I may say to him, "Get away from me. Can't you see that I am tired and can't talk." The Lord Jesus, however, when He was in the most excruciating pain, did not turn away this person, but showed him acceptance and love, and assured him about his future after death[45].

The feeling of acceptance gives a sense of safety

This sense of acceptance gives a person rest and makes him feel at peace inwardly, that he is accepted and loved. I sometimes say to the church congregation

---

42   Ibid.

43   See Luke 23:39–43.

44   Luke 23:43.

45   Literally: his eternity.

that when you hear that a woman has recently moved in, and she is living around the church, you visit and get introduced to this new-comer. You ask about who she is, how she lives and how is she like?. You are told that she has been married and divorced five times, and she is currently living with a man [who is] not her husband. So how many of you will welcome her? How many of you would like to deal with a woman like this? You, undoubtedly, know the woman I mean. It is the Samaritan woman who went to the well at noon to fill her waterpot. Why did she go to the well at this time specifically, when it is very hot, knowing that the best time to go to the well is either early morning or at sunset? She used to go at noon, in the extreme heat, to avoid being seen by people, because she felt rejected.

But luckily for her, she found a person sitting at the well, waiting for her. To begin with, she did not want to deal with him, wishing to avoid him. Jesus said to her, "Give Me a drink." Then the Samaritan woman said to Him, "How is it that You, being a Jew, ask a drink from me, a Samaritan woman?"[46] She, as though, wants to say to Him, "Mind Your own business and leave me alone. Let me fill my waterpot and get going." This defensiveness by her is a sort of a wall she wanted to hide behind. And this was a sort of "fig leaves" she wanted to disappear behind. And perhaps she was thinking that this person, after talking with her and knowing

---

46   See John 4:1–42.

everything about her life, would reject her.

But the Lord Christ began talking with her, saying, "You have well said, 'I have no husband,' for you have had five husbands, and the one whom you now have is not your husband; in that you spoke truly."[47] At this, she felt accepted, and this feeling transformed the Samaritan into a preacher to all the people of Samaria. She did not care about what the people would say about her [any longer], and her testimony was, "Come, see a Man who told me all things that I ever did,"[48] and she was not afraid to be asked by the people, "What did you do?"

The feeling of being accepted liberated her and smashed the fetters with which she was living, being bound with the shackles of fear. She was transformed into a missionary. Therefore, when we reject others, we bind them with fetters, but when we show them true love, these fetters will be smashed and we will live in the true freedom.

So, the sense of being accepted gives also a sense of safety, and this sense makes the husband and wife exchange their opinions and discuss their disagreements in an atmosphere of love and honesty.

God's acceptance of us, and our acceptance of one another

We have to display God's acceptance of us to all

---

47   John 4:17–18.
48   John 4:29.

people around us, and this, through our acceptance of one another. By this, God is glorified in our life. Paul the Apostle says, "Therefore receive[49] one another, just as Christ also received us, to the glory of God."[50] What does he mean by saying, "to the glory of God"? The Apostle wants to say, "Accepting each other gives God the glory." How can this be done, and it is difficult to accept the other, unless I feel God's acceptance of me? But when I am sure that God loves me and accepts me as I am, this makes me reflect this acceptance by my acceptance of others. And when people see that Christians love each other with a sincere, true love, and accept each other, they glorify God who is present in their midst.

If we realize our shortcomings, and that we are imperfect, and despite this, we are accepted by others, [then] it becomes easier for us to accept each other.

I would like to emphasize this important point which helps us to accept each other. When I know that [although] I am an imperfect person and have many shortcomings, yet I pursue the others' acceptance of me, consequently I have to, likewise, accept the other [person] despite their shortcomings and weaknesses. This is especially [the case] if I have made a covenant with the other before the altar in the Mystery of holy matrimony.

---

49 The word in the Arabic verse may be translated into "accept," but it appears as "receive" in NKJV.

50 Romans 15:7.

In conclusion, there is an important question, after we have talked about these six feelings or needs: if a problem or a fight occurs between the husband and wife, how do we know that this problem occurred as a consequence of hidden feelings or not? This leads us to another subject, that is, the external signs of the hidden feelings.

3

The External Signs of the Hidden Feelings

There are four things that help us realize whether the problem occurred because of hidden feelings or not.

First: The Magnitude of the Problem is Greater Than the Event

What happened between a husband and his wife could be trivial, yet the problem resulting from it is very big. Frequently I hear married couples say to me, "Your Grace, we do not know the reason for which we had a fight," or, "We do not have issues[51] we fight over. All our fights occur because of insignificant matters." When we hear such words, we must immediately realize that the reason

---

51 Or: subjects.

is underlying needs in both side which are not satisfied. There may be one or more of the six needs we have previously talked about.

Second: Talking About the Same Issue with No Avail

The second sign [helping us] know if the problem which took place resulted from hidden feelings, is when you find yourself talking about the same issue continually without reaching a solution. For example, the husband and wife may continue for ten years talking about the issue of money. And this issue may be a cause of continual disagreements between them. Also, they may receive a counsel from a priest, and yet there is no solution for this problem.

The problem does not lie in the issue of money, but it essentially issues from fear of love of control. There may be a hidden need we need to discover and talk about. The husband may have a desire to have the upper hand, and therefore he does not want to give her the money she asks for; the wife may have a fear that her husband is controlling her, and this fear may be the result of an experience she went through in the past when she was young.

Third: Evading the Discussion or Avoiding the Other

One side may avoid going into a dialogue and discussion. Someone may reveal that there is something he is uncomfortable with and may want to talk about it frankly, but the other person may evade having a dialogue about it. And this may be in many forms. It may be in the form of hasty agreement, meaning that the husband may say to his wife, "Okay, what is it you want to discuss?" So she may say, "We can discuss this and that [matter]." He responds immediately, saying, "I agree with whatever you say." But in reality he does not agree, but wants to end the conversation quickly, and does not want to delve into the details of the issue of the discussion.

Also, when one side avoids talking about an issue, it may be because of the fear of rejection, for he may feel that he will be rejected if he says something. Or it may be that he does not want to give up something within him. He wants to have authority; therefore, he is not ready to give up this thing.

Another reason for refusing to have a dialogue is a past trauma the husband suffered because of lack of acceptance or appreciation; therefore, his sense of honor and self-esteem dot not permit him to be able to have a discussion and dialogue, because he considers that [having a] dialogue [shows] weakness.

Fourth: Retaining and Keeping a Record

For example, a wife may accuse her husband of having forgotten her birthday, so her husband gets her a gift, but he says to her, "Remember this, so that you do not come afterward and say to me, 'You have forgotten my birthday.'" When their wedding anniversary comes, he gets her a gift also, and says to her, "Do not say I have forgotten our wedding anniversary!" Giving the gift in this way—"Here is a gift, eh!"—indicates that he has a feeling that his wife has doubts about his integrity and commitment, and consequently, he keeps a record of the event (giving a gift) so that he may defend his integrity; or it may be so that he can prove that the other person is controlling him.

Another example, a wife may say to her husband, "You have promised before the priest that you would give me a certain monthly amount [of money] to cover my needs and the household needs. A month has passed by and you have given me nothing, and another [has passed] and you have not given me [anything]." She begins keeping a record of what is going on, the reason being her fear of his control and power.

A third example, a husband, who is not committed to the marital covenant, may say that he has done this and that, and begins defending himself, before anybody accuses him of being not committed to the marital covenant.

These four manifestations indicate the presence of hidden needs that are not satisfied, about which we do not talk with frankness, love and transparency. If one or more of these four things takes place, we have to realize that one of the deep needs has to be satisfied.

Do not focus in the beginning on solutions, but on understanding the other

I would like to reiterate an advice I previously mentioned in the beginning of this topic: when you start talking about the hidden feelings or needs, do not hasten immediately to find solutions.

Take, however, a considerable time to listen and understand the other, because by this, you satisfy a need in him of being accepted. You have to make him feel that you accept him, understand him, and are listening to him. We sometimes want to offer quick solutions so as to end the issue, but, nevertheless, we do not feel at peace[52]. Therefore, when discussing our inner deep needs, we have to focus on understanding the other side. Focus on the way of accepting the other, and how you may understand the issue from his point of view, and not your own point of view. This understanding is sometimes itself the solution of the problem.

> *"If you have God, then you have everything, even though you are deprived of everything. And if you do not have God, then you are deprived of everything, even though you possess everything."*

> —Saint Anthony—

---

52   Literally: at rest.

4

Christ is He Who Satisfies

I would like to draw your attention to this very important matter, that Jesus Christ is the One who satisfies all our needs. The more you are satisfied by Christ, the more you can satisfy others. Also, your satisfaction by the Lord Christ will make up for any deficiency the other [person] does not fulfill.

There is a maxim that says, "The person who lacks something cannot give it." You cannot satisfy the other's needs, if you [yourself] are not satisfied by Christ and [if you] are not delighted in Him first. Your satisfaction by Christ will make up for any deficiency the other cannot fulfill. No matter how perfect we may be, we cannot satisfy each other's [needs] fully, for we cannot fulfill all the needs of each other.

The Lord Christ, however, being God and perfect by nature, is able to satisfy us completely. He loved us with an infinite and unconditional love, with a volitional and sacrificial love.

Therefore, He is able to fulfill all our needs by the attributes of His love, the unlimited, infinite, unconditional, and He loved us by His own will and sacrificed Himself for our sake.

The love of Christ casts out fear from our hearts

There is no fear in love; but perfect love casts out fear, because fear involves torment. But he who fears has not been made perfect in love. [53]

Because of this love, we are not afraid of God; I do not mean by this the fear of God, but the fear servants[54] have. God loves us, and in no way would He reject us. Therefore, when a person feels that he has gotten into a predicament for some reason, you find him go into his room easily, cry before the Lord, and confess all his sins to Him. This happens for two reasons:

The first reason: His knowledge that God knows about all that he did, for "I, the LORD, search the heart, I test the mind,"[55] "and there is no creature hidden from His sight, but all things are naked and open to the eyes of Him to whom we must give

---

53   1 John 4:18.

54   Literally: slaves.

55   Jeremiah 17:10.

account."[56]

The second reason: His feeling of God's marvelous love for him, and that He will accept him. But this does not justify that we be content with this, and consequently we do not go to our father of confession, because confession before the priest makes a person feel a shame that helps him toward repentance.

What I would like to say here is that the love of God makes a person throw himself into the bosoms of God without fear, and this is what made David the Prophet say, "Please let us fall into the hand of the LORD, for His mercies are great; but do not let me fall into the hand of man."[57]

Christ has satisfied our six needs

First: Did the Lord Christ come to have authority over us? Are we afraid of God's authority over us? I would like to meditate, together [with you], on what came in the Gospel according to St. Matthew:

> But Jesus called them to Himself and said, "You know that the rulers of the Gentiles lord it over them, and those who are great exercise authority over them. Yet it shall not be so among you; but whoever desires to become great among you, let him be your

---

56 Hebrews 4:13.

57 2 Samuel 24:14.

servant. And whoever desires to be first among you, let him be your slave—just as the Son of Man did not come to be served, but to serve, and to give His life a ransom for many."[58]

How wonderful! Who of us is able to imagine, after [reading] this, that the Lord came to prevail and have authority over us? He said, "I have not come like the rulers of the world and the great who exercise authority over you, but I have come so that I may serve you, and not so that you may serve Me." Therefore, there is no fear in our relationship with God; no fear at all that He will exercise control over us, but He gave us the freedom [to choose] to live with Him or to reject Him. He gave us the freedom to even sin before Him. He gave us the freedom to even deny His existence.

Second: God does not desire to have authority over us, but came to serve us with all love and humility. You will not find anyone who cares about us, and who fulfills our need for love and care and attention like God. The Lord Jesus says, "As the Father loved Me, I also have loved You; abide in My love."[59] What is the measure of Your love for us, Lord? "Greater love has no one then this, than to lay down one's life for his friends."[60] Is there a greater love than the love of Him who shed His blood on

58   Matthew 20:25–28.

59   John 15:9.

60   John 15:13.

the cross for our sakes? Therefore, I declare and profess that there is no one ever, who loves me with a greater love than the love of Christ who gave himself for my sake.

Third: The Lord Jesus, also, appreciates us, as evidenced from His letting us be His fellow workers[61]. Sometimes when I think about service, I feel that I am negligent in the service because of my weaknesses. So I imagine that God wants to serve people, but is God not able to serve the world Himself without needing anyone of us? Yes, He is able to, but He will even be immeasurably better [at doing the work Himself] than all of us. Also, we may be the cause of crippling the service because of our weaknesses and sins. Nevertheless, the Lord Christ appreciates us so much that he makes us His fellow workers in the service, though He does not need us at all. Yet He says, "As You sent Me into the world, I also have sent them into the world."[62] This means that God appreciates our labor and effort, and wants us to be His fellow workers, even though we, actually, cripple His work in the creation.

Let us meditate on His occurrences with Abraham and Moses, of which we have spoken earlier. For who is Abraham that he should stand before God and negotiate with Him? And who is Moses that he should stand before the Lord and say,

---

61   Literally: He lets us be sharers with Him in the work.

62   John 17:18.

"If You destroy them, then blot out my name from the book of life."[63] In a nutshell, I can satisfy my need for appreciation through my relationship with God.

Fourth: [As to] the need of commitment, God has promised that He will not leave us. Do we fear that God will leave us? No, not at all, "indeed, let God be true but every man a liar."[64] Meditate on what the Holy Spirit said:

> Let your conduct be without covetousness; be content with such things as you have. For He Himself has said, "I will never leave you nor forsake you." So we may boldly say: "The Lord is my helper; I will not fear. What can man do to me?"[65]

We can depend on our relationship with God, and on His promise to us that "I will never leave you nor forsake you."

He also said to us, "And lo, I am with you always, even to the end of the age."[66]

God will never leave us, and will never leave us to drown, but on the contrary, even if we ourselves leave God and [then] return to Him at any moment, we will find His arms open to us, as it happened

---

63   See Exodus 32:32.

64   Romans 3:4.

65   Hebrews 13:5–6.

66   Matthew 28:20.

with the prodigal son.[67]

Fifth: [As to] the need of uprightness and integrity, we are able to hide our intentions and motives from others, and I am able to appear contrary to who I really am, but God tests the hearts and minds[68]. And as David said, "O LORD, You have searched me and known me. You know my sitting down and my rising up; You understand my thought afar off. You comprehend my path and my lying down, and are acquainted with all my ways. For there is not a word on my tongue, but behold, O LORD, You know it altogether."[69]

God knows everything about us, and despite His knowledge of all that is in us, He has not changed His love for us. He knew the Samaritan woman inside out[70], and likewise He knew the right-hand thief, [yet] His love for him was not changed, and His love for us also has not been changed.

Sixth: God accepts us with all love, accepts us as we are, with all our sins and weaknesses. And because He loves us, He helps us to offer repentance for our sins and weaknesses, and makes us live in righteousness and godliness before Him, and He says to us:

---

67   See Luke 15:20.

68   Psalm 7:9.

69   Psalm 139:1–4.

70   Literally: He knew what was within and without the Samaritan woman.

No longer do I call you servants, for a servant does not know what his master is doing; but I have called you friends, for all things that I heard from My Father I have made known to you. You did not choose Me, but I chose you and appointed you that you should go and bear fruit, and that your fruit should remain, that whatever you ask the Father in My name He may give you.[71]

The Lord Christ says to me, "No longer do I call you servant, but I have called you My beloved. You are my friend because I have told you, informed you, and shared with you all that I heard from My Father."

In conclusion, through my relationship with the Lord Jesus Christ, God is able to satisfy all these six needs in me.

He will make me feel that He appreciates me, and that He appreciates the service I offer Him; He will make me feel loved and accepted, and [satisfy the need for] commitment also, according to His true promise, "I will never leave you nor forsake you."[72] He also fulfills my need for uprightness, even though He perfectly knows me in truth, but despite this He does not change His love and His acceptance toward me, and He deals with me as a person who is dearly beloved to Him. Therefore, He

---

71 John 15:15–16.
72 Hebrews 13:5.

says, "You did not choose Me, but I chose you."[73]

When these needs are fulfilled, and are satisfied through our relationship with God, we are, consequently, able to fulfill and satisfy them for other people.

I pray that the Lord may complete whatever is missing in these needs if they were not satisfied in you. To Him be all glory forever. Amen.

---

73   John 15:16.